JUNIOR SONGSCAPE
CHILDREN'S FAVOURITES

20 classic children's songs

arranged by Lin Marsh

with online audio and downloadable lyrics

Especially for Alfie and Thomas

This edition © 2008 by Faber Music Ltd
First published in 2008 by Faber Music Ltd
Bloomsbury House
74–77 Great Russell Street
London WC1B 3DA
Cover by Lydia Merrills-Ashcroft
Design by Susan Clarke
Movement notes by Wendy Cook
Music processed by Cotswold Music Typesetting
Printed in England by Caligraving Ltd
All rights reserved

ISBN10: 0-571-52644-6
EAN13: 978-0-571-52644-4

Audio recorded in BatMusic Studio, Surrey, June 2008
Singers: Lin Marsh and Dominic Marsh
Backings created and engineered by Ben Tompsett
Producer: Leigh Rumsey
℗ 2008 Faber Music Ltd © 2008 Faber Music Ltd

To buy Faber Music publications or to find out about the full range of titles available please contact your local retailer or Faber Music sales enquiries:

Faber Music Limited, Burnt Mill, Elizabeth Way, Harlow CM20 2HX England
Tel: +44 (0) 1279 82 89 82   Fax: +44 (0) 1279 82 89 83
sales@fabermusic.com   fabermusicstore.com

Contents

	full version	backing version	
Heigh-ho Frank Churchill & Larry Morey	Folder 1 · 1	Folder 1 · 2	page 5
The Sun Has Got His Hat On Ralph Butler & Noel Gay	Folder 1 · 3	Folder 1 · 4	page 8
Whistle While You Work Frank Churchill & Larry Morey	Folder 1 · 5	Folder 1 · 6	page 10
How Much is that Doggie in the Window? Bob Merrill	Folder 1 · 7	Folder 1 · 8	page 12
Busy Doing Nothing Jimmy Van Heusen & Johnny Burke	Folder 1 · 9	Folder 1 · 10	page 15
Sing a Rainbow Arthur Hamilton	Folder 1 · 11	Folder 1 · 12	page 18
Who's Afraid of the Big Bad Wolf? Frank Churchill & Ann Ronell	Folder 1 · 13	Folder 1 · 14	page 20
Little April Shower Frank Churchill & Larry Morey	Folder 1 · 15	Folder 1 · 16	page 23
The Hippopotamus Song Michael Flanders & Donald Swann	Folder 1 · 17	Folder 1 · 18	page 26
Feed the Birds Richard Sherman & Robert Sherman	Folder 1 · 19	Folder 1 · 20	page 29
Dingle Dangle Scarecrow Geoffrey Russell-Smith & Mollie Russell-Smith	Folder 2 · 1	Folder 2 · 2	page 32
Puff (The Magic Dragon) Peter Yarrow & Leonard Lipton	Folder 2 · 3	Folder 2 · 4	page 33
The Teddy Bears' Picnic John W. Bratton & Jimmy Kennedy	Folder 2 · 5	Folder 2 · 6	page 36
Nellie the Elephant Ralph Butler & Peter Hart	Folder 2 · 7	Folder 2 · 8	page 42
Going to the Zoo Tom Paxton	Folder 2 · 9	Folder 2 · 10	page 46
The Runaway Train Carson Robison & Robert Massey	Folder 2 · 11	Folder 2 · 12	page 49
Swinging on a Star Jimmy Van Heusen & Johnny Burke	Folder 2 · 13	Folder 2 · 14	page 52
Two Little Men in a Flying Saucer Arthur Pitt	Folder 2 · 15	Folder 2 · 16	page 55
Morningtown Ride Malvina Reynolds	Folder 2 · 17	Folder 2 · 18	page 58
Give a Little Whistle Leigh Harline & Ned Washington	Folder 2 · 19	Folder 2 · 20	page 61

Using the online audio

For online audio scan the QR code or go to fabermusic.com/content/audio.
Lyrics for most of these songs* can be downloaded from the product page on fabermusicstore.com.

* Lyrics to four songs are not included due to copyright restrictions

Suggestions for adding movement

Children's enjoyment of movement and music is apparent from very early in their lives. They enthusiastically clap, sway, stretch and bounce to tunes and rhythms, making natural links between sound and physical movement. This colourful collection of songs offers a wide range of possibilities for movement including dance, mime and lively, expressive use of faces.

Here are some suggestions for getting things started, but you will find the children will have lots of ideas of their own.

- Establish the mood of a song
- Explore the structure, for example, is there a chorus that is repeated? Identify any story running through the song
- Who is the song about? Me? Us? Me and someone from my family? Imaginary characters? Animals?
- Emphasize rhythms through simple repetition
- Underline any action words
- Underline 'feeling' words, for example 'happy' or 'afraid'

Songs that tell a story

Puff the Magic Dragon Create a dream-like, fantasy atmosphere. Use images of the sea and pirate ships, cave-dwelling, princes and kings bowing to Puff, with Jackie looking out or riding on his tail. Explore big and small in movement and body shape for the two main characters.

Nellie the Elephant Show Nellie packing and waving goodbye. Use the rhythm of 'trumpety trump, trump, trump, trump' moving feet on the spot, with hands beating thighs or chest for Nellie's journey. Arms and hands can show Nellie's big ears flapping, and hearing the call of the Head of the Herd (freeze and focus eyes and posture on an agreed point).

Who's Afraid of the Big Bad Wolf? The three pigs build their houses with different materials, two celebrating with flute and fiddle, and the third one having to work much harder, so no time for fun. Follow the events in the story and explore actions such as collapsing, disintegrating, resisting, sliding. Have a brave posture for the chorus – chest out, head high – and a sneaky posture for the Wolf!

The Teddy Bears' Picnic There are two roles in this song: You, the watcher, being very careful and quiet, and the Teddy bears dancing in a circle at their picnic and playing hide and seek amongst the trees.

Going To The Zoo Eager faces anticipating an exciting day at the start and end of this song will establish the mood. It's about 'us' – use lots of eye contact from you and between the children. Create the animal characters in the middle verses, and have lots of yawning and nodding on the return journey.

Songs about characters

Feed the Birds Choose some children to portray the bird woman moving calmly through the group, giving out bags of crumbs to be sprinkled on the hands of the others held out for the birds. Focus up and out to create the presence of the birds.

Two Little Men in a Flying Saucer are aliens from another planet visiting earth. Try this in a class circle (earth) with two children as the aliens moving around and in and out of those in the circle. Or turn your two hands into the little men in their saucer, and let them fly around your own body – above, behind, to the sides and so on.

In **The Sun Has Got His Hat On** we can all be the Sun! Use simple actions as suggested in the song – putting on a hat during the introduction, cheering using arms, opening out to a wide shape, jumping and smiling.

How Much is that Doggie in the Window? Use of eyes and focus to express longing for a dog are absolutely essential. You can be the pet shopkeeper they need to persuade.

In **Dingle dangle scarecrow** children crouch down with eyes closed for cows sleeping and hens roosting. At 'Up jumped the scarecrow' they jump up and dance on the spot from side to side, wagging their heads for 'a flippy floppy hat', then shaking their hands and feet. Encourage looseness in the feet and ankles, but point out that balance is essential since scarecrows are no use if they fall on the floor!

The Runaway Train The choruses of this hazardous journey use the rhythm of the train on the tracks as it races along. Use arms like pistons to depict this mechanical creature.

Morningtown Ride A different type of journey takes place on this train! Explore relaxed body positions – sitting, standing and lying as you sing this dreamy song. Can you roll gently from one side to the other, rocking and rolling and singing?

In **The Hippopotamus Song** the chorus depicts a large wallowing character whose favourite place is a mud pool. Explore weighty movement with lots of 'slooping' and 'glooping' as Hippo extracts himself from the sticky mud. The verses tell the story: use faces in an animated way.

Songs about the natural world

Sing a Rainbow creates a colourful image; locate the rainbow in your working space and encourage the children to see it in their imaginations, and show you where it is with clear focus. Emphasise that it is an arc, so it has two ends nearer the ground and the centre arches up into the sky.

Little April Shower is a delicate song whose repeated phrase of 'drip, drip, drop' holds the key to its quality. You might use very light dabbing movements of the fingers to illustrate the rhythm and meaning of these words.

Songs about making you feel better

Concentrate on the message of these songs. Children can sing them to an audience, or to each other, with or without simple actions based on action words in the songs. The laid-back feel of **Swinging On a Star** contrasts nicely with the energetic **Heigh-Ho**. **Busy Doing Nothing** can be contrasted with **Whistle While You Work**, which contains a wonderful list of work to be done, with opportunities for mime or movement. **Give a Little Whistle** is probably the ultimate 'cheer up' song! Attempts to whistle will definitely produce hilarity – excellent for a dark winter day.

Wendy Cook

Heigh-Ho

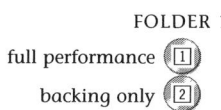

Words by Larry Morey
Music by Frank Churchill

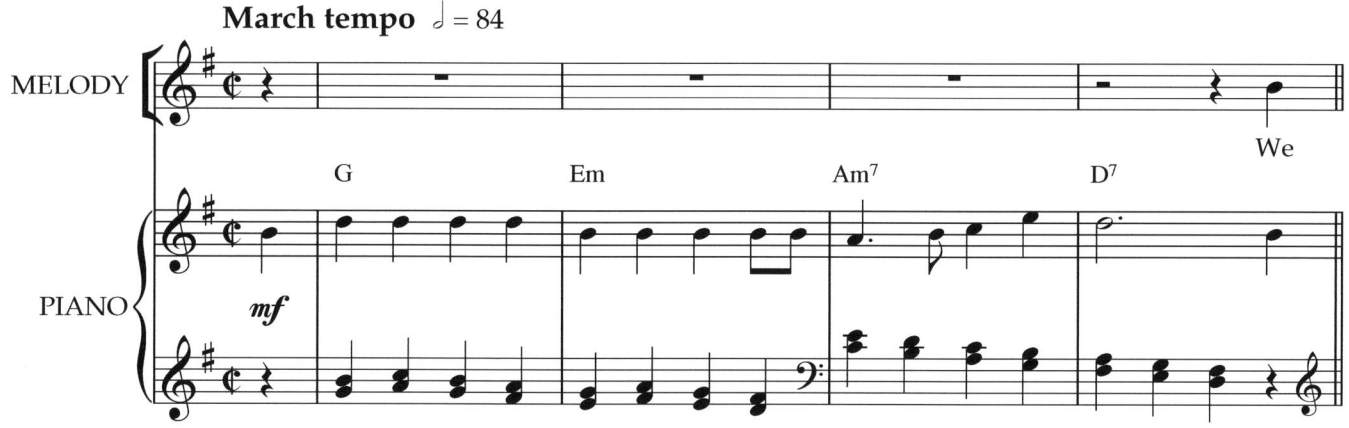

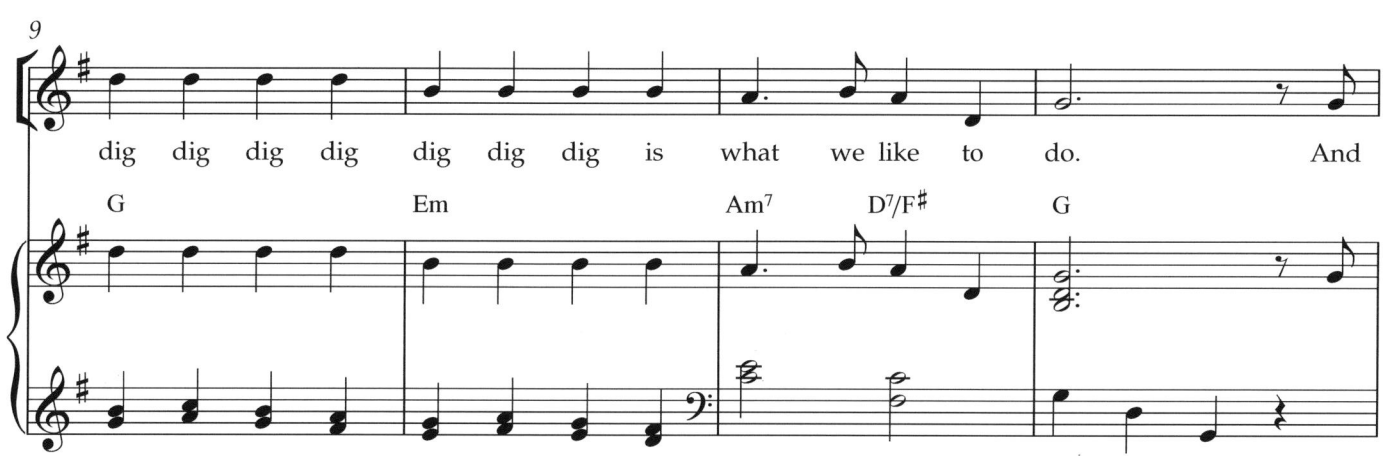

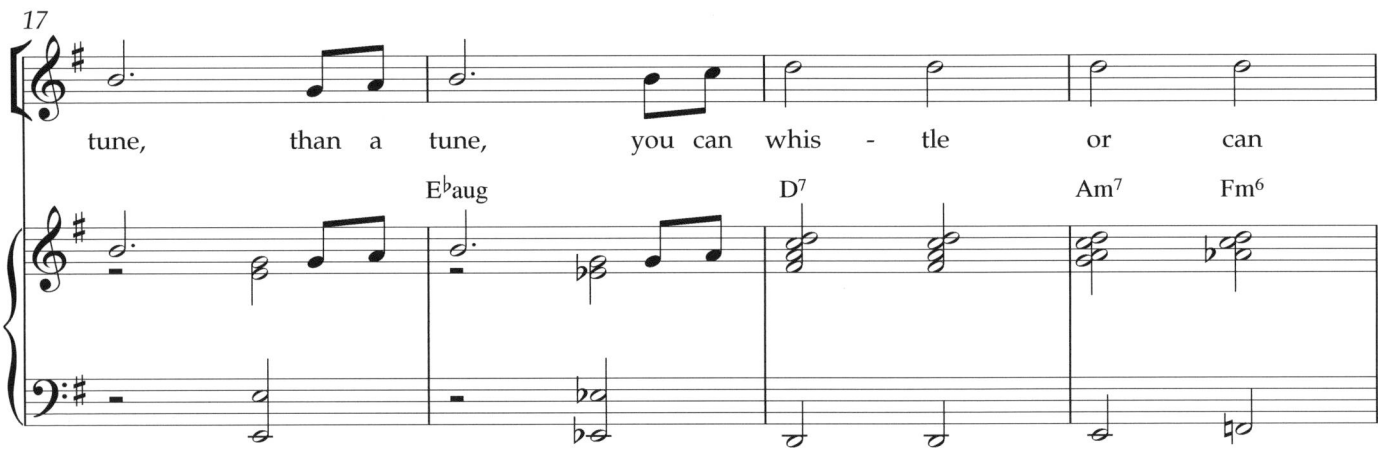
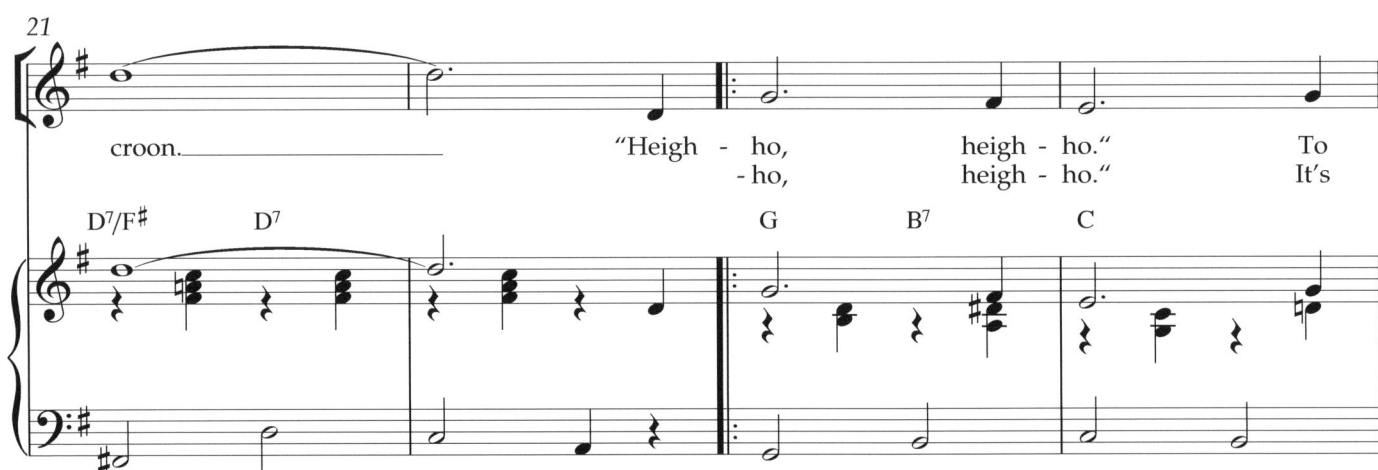

8
FOLDER 1
full performance [3]
backing only [4]

The Sun Has Got His Hat On

Words and Music by
Ralph Butler and Noel Gay
arr. Lin Marsh

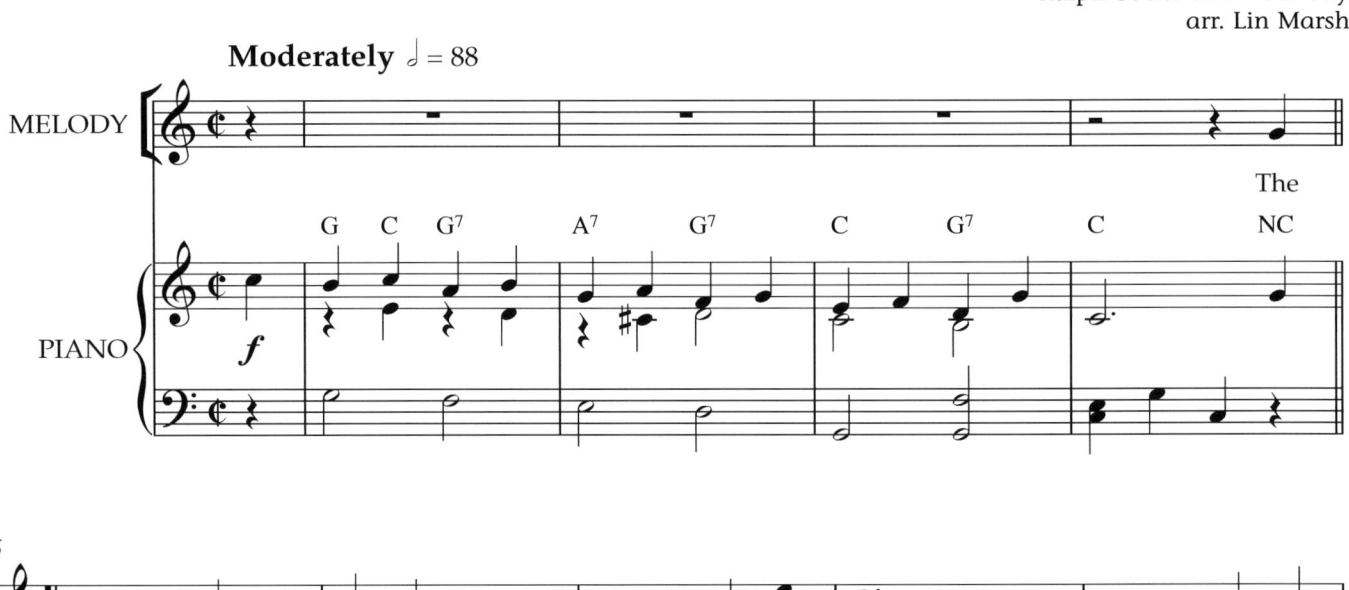

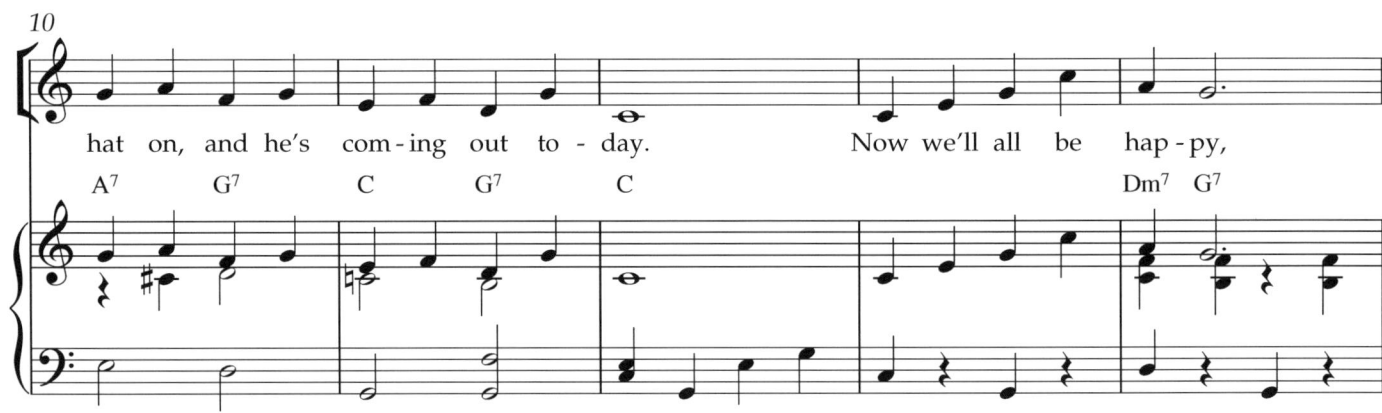

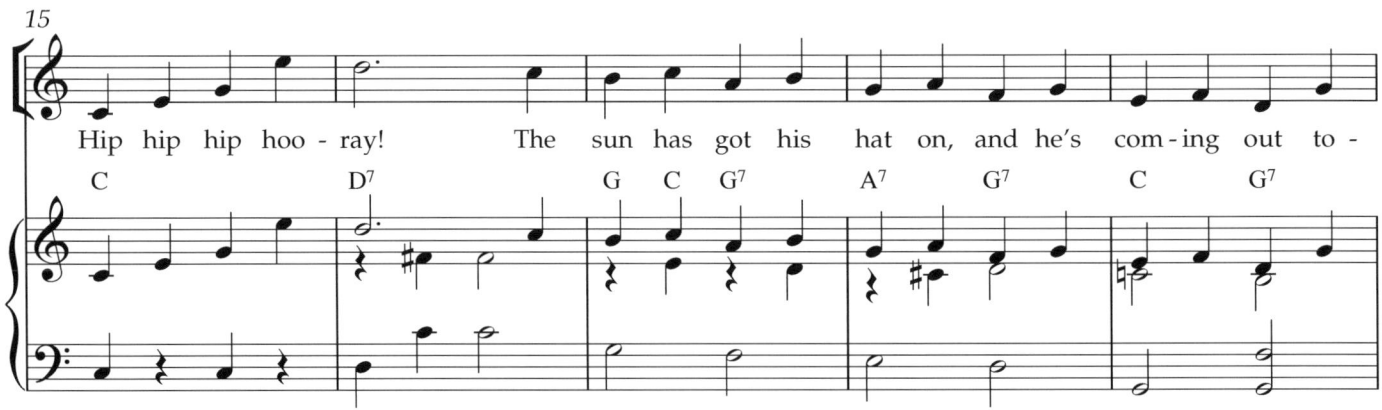

© 1932 West's Ltd and Estate Music Co Ltd
B Feldman & Co Ltd and Richard Armitage Ltd

Whistle While You Work

Words by Larry Morey
Music by Frank Churchill

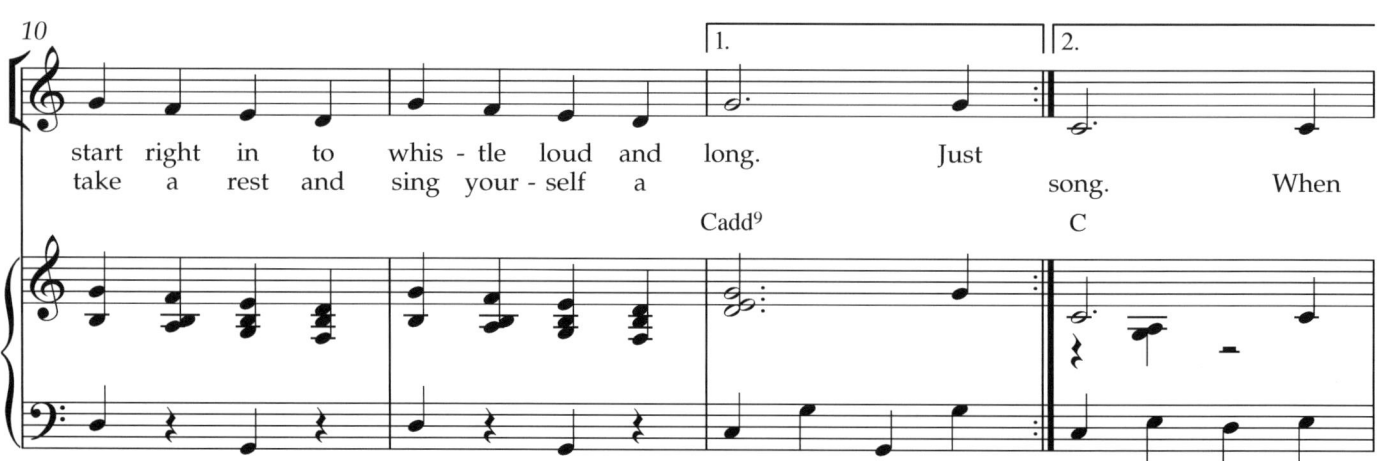

© 1937 Bourne Co.
Copyright Renewed
This Arrangement © Copyright 2008 by Bourne Co.
All Rights Reserved International Copyright Secured

Busy Doing Nothing

FOLDER 1
full performance [9]
backing only [10]

Words by Johnny Burke
Music by James van Heusen
arr. Lin Marsh

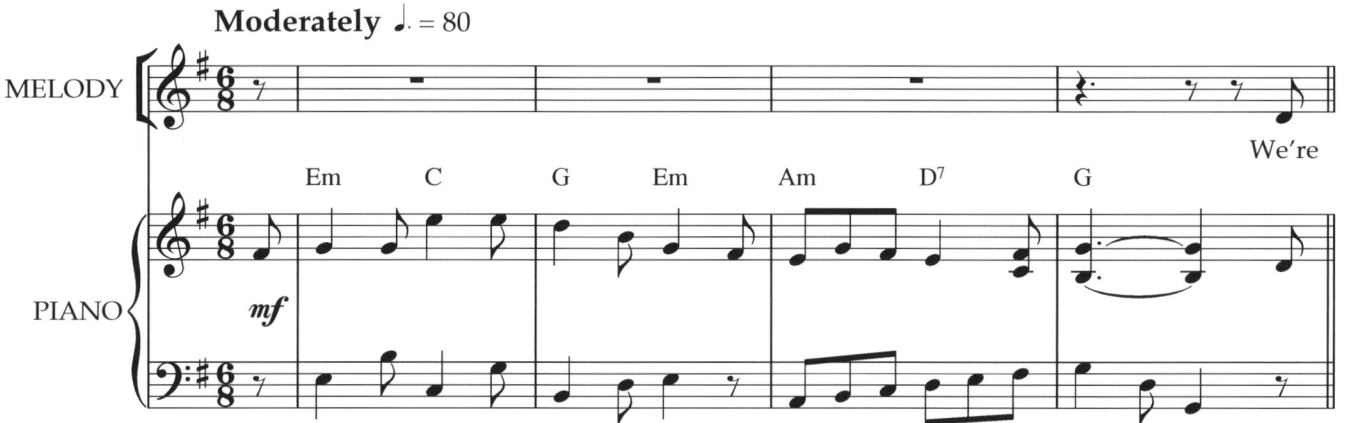
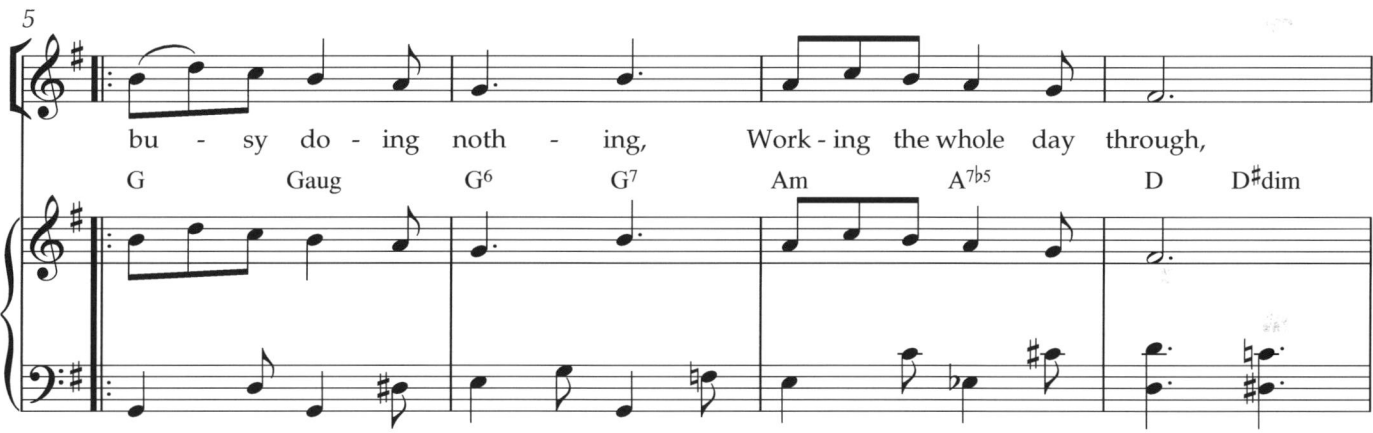
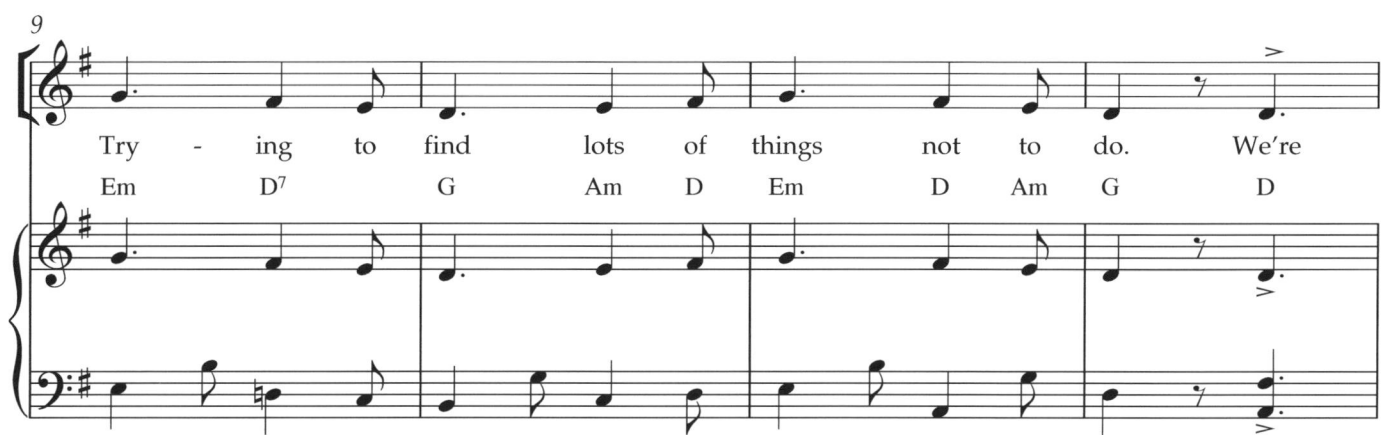

© 1957 Burke-Van-Heusen Inc
Chappell Morris Ltd

18 FOLDER 1
full performance [11]
backing only [12]

Sing a Rainbow

Words and Music by Arthur Hamilton
arr. Lin Marsh

© 1955 (Renewed) Mark VII Ltd
Warner/Chappell North America Ltd

Who's Afraid of the Big Bad Wolf?

Words and Music by Frank Churchill
Additional lyric by Ann Ronell

© 1933 Bourne Co.
Copyright Renewed
This Arrangement © Copyright 2008 by Bourne Co.
All Rights Reserved International Copyright Secured

FOLDER 1
full performance 15
backing only 16

Little April Shower

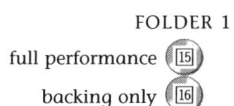

Words by Larry Morey
Music by Frank Churchill

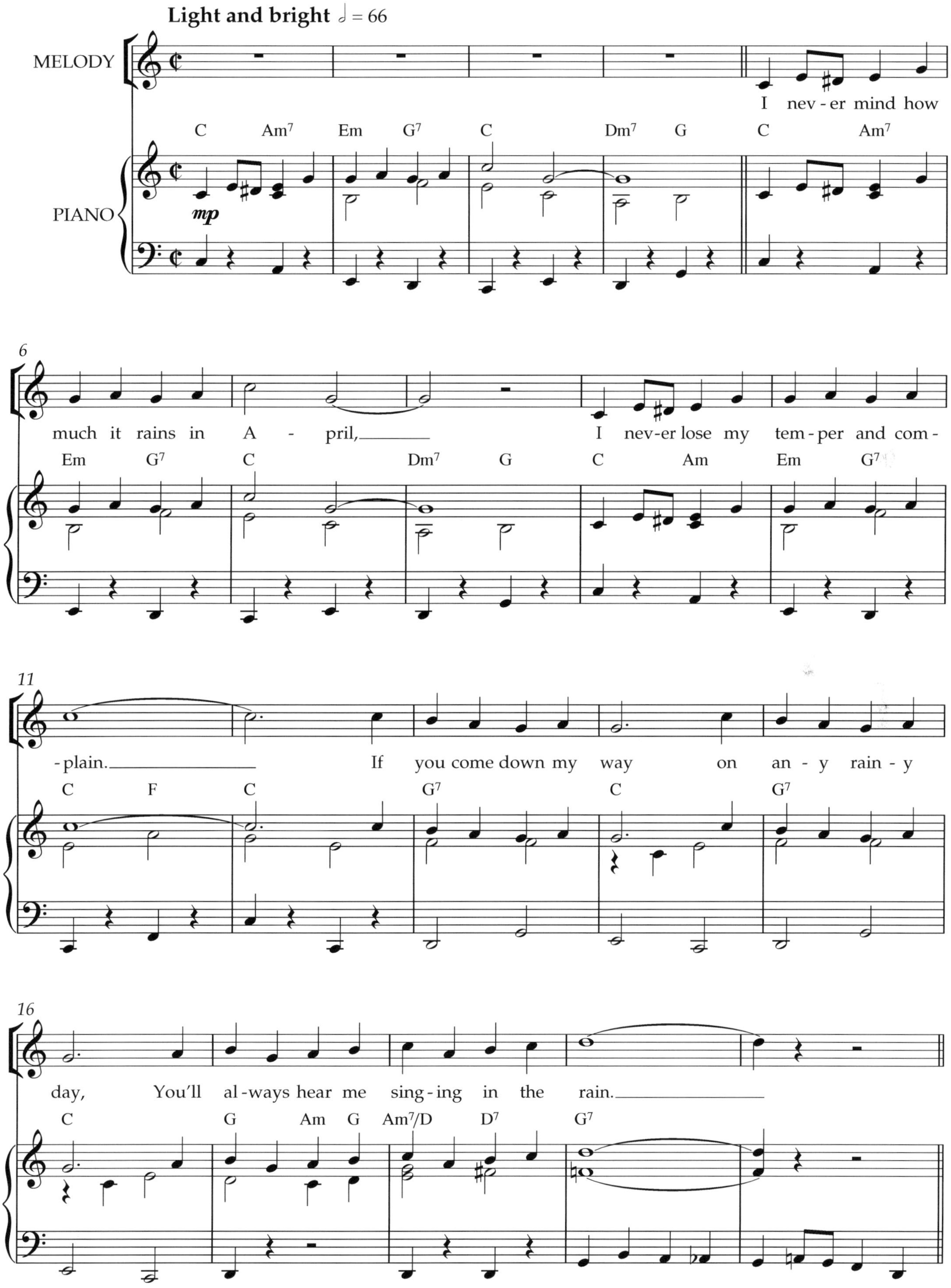

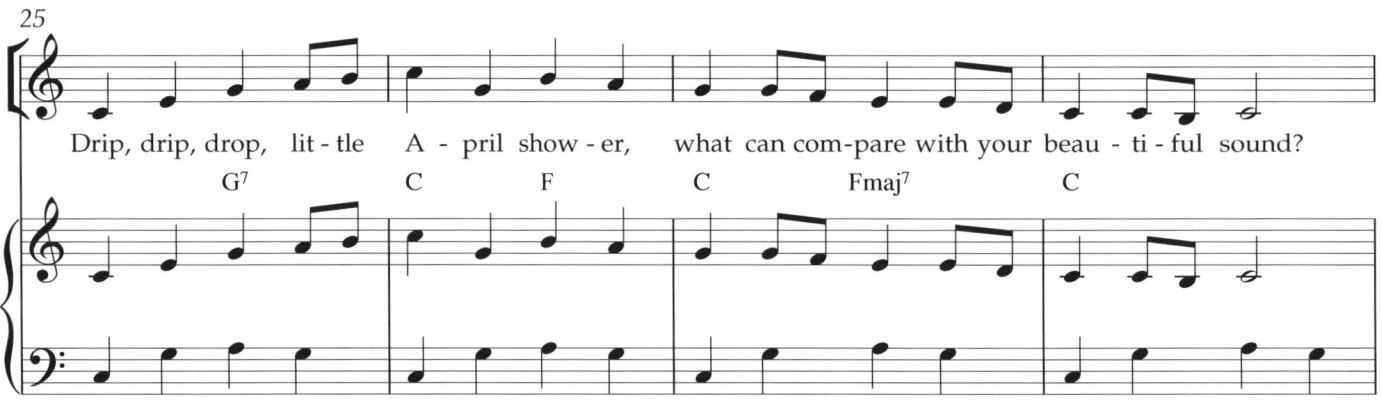

The Hippopotamus Song

Words by Michael Flanders
Music by Donald Swann
arr. Lin Marsh

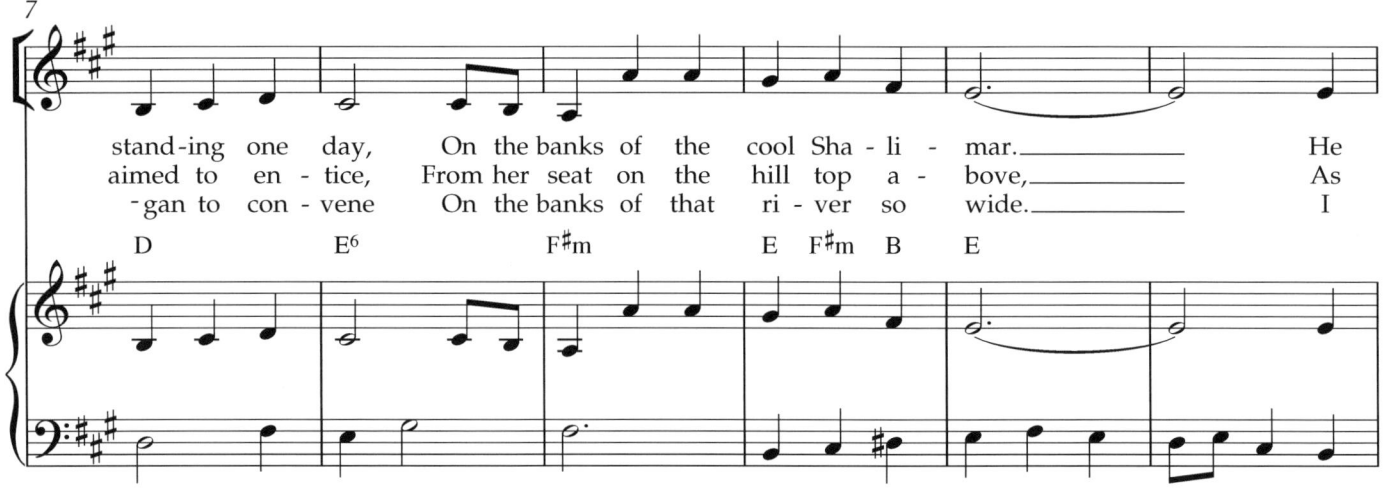

1. A bold Hip-po-pot-a-mus was standing one day, On the banks of the cool Sha-li-mar. He
(2.) fair Hip-po-pot-a-ma he aimed to en-tice, From her seat on the hill top a-bove, As
(3.) more Hip-po-pot-a-mi be-gan to con-vene On the banks of that ri-ver so wide. I

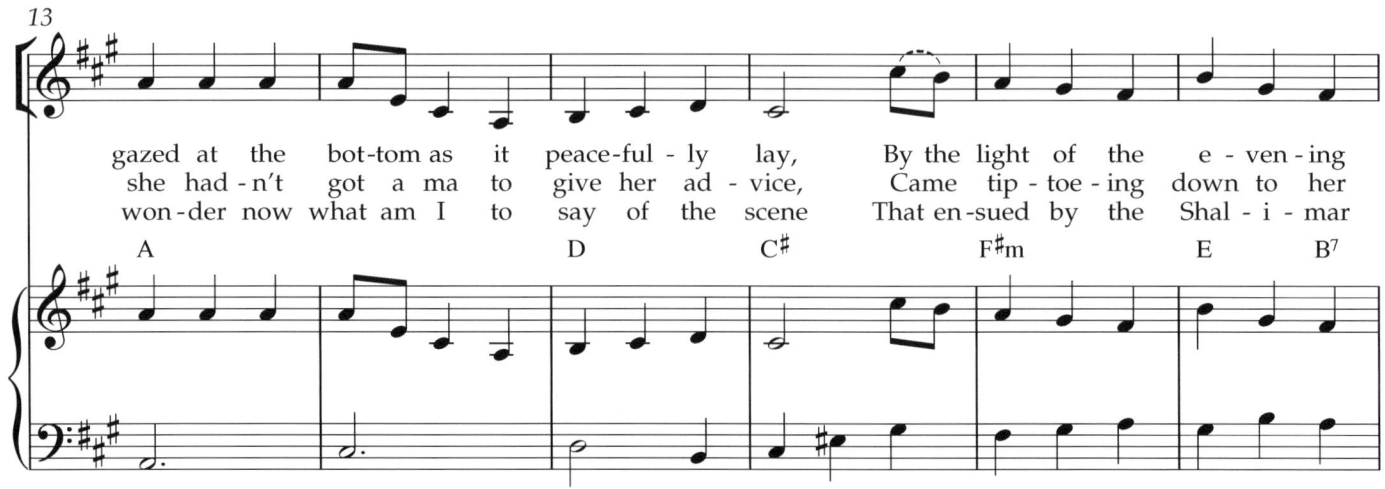

gazed at the bot-tom as it peace-ful-ly lay, By the light of the e-ven-ing
she had-n't got a ma to give her ad-vice, Came tip-toe-ing down to her
won-der now what am I to say of the scene That en-sued by the Shal-i-mar

© 1952 Chappell Music Ltd

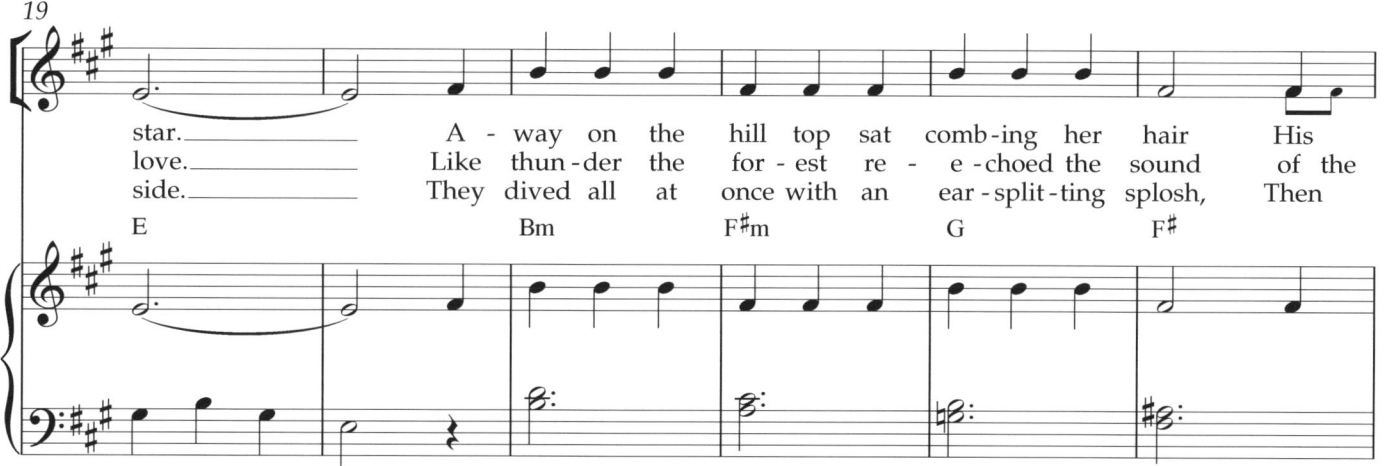
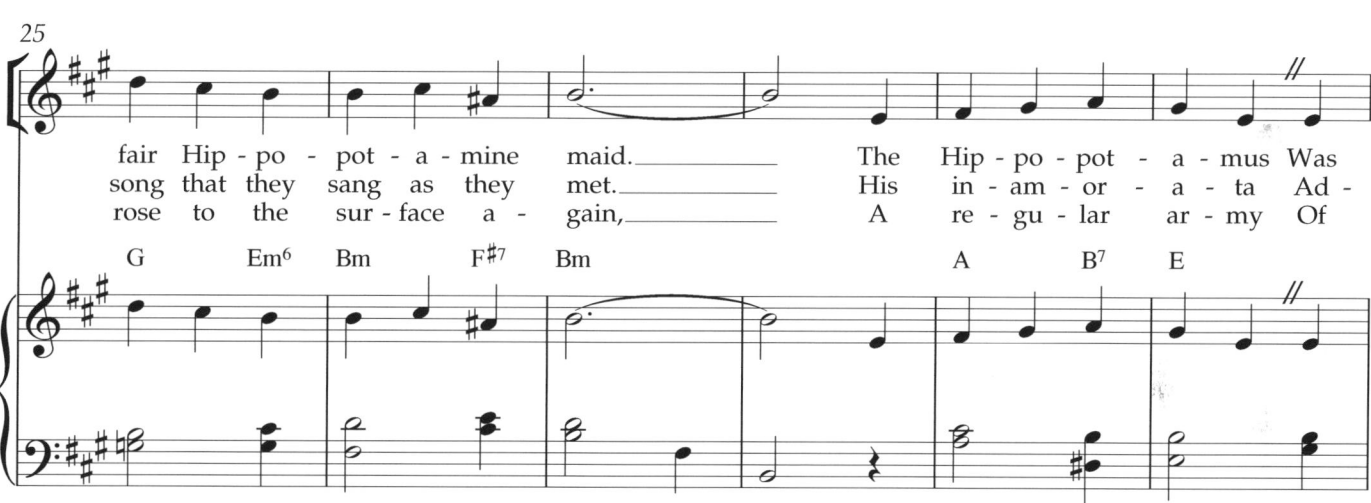
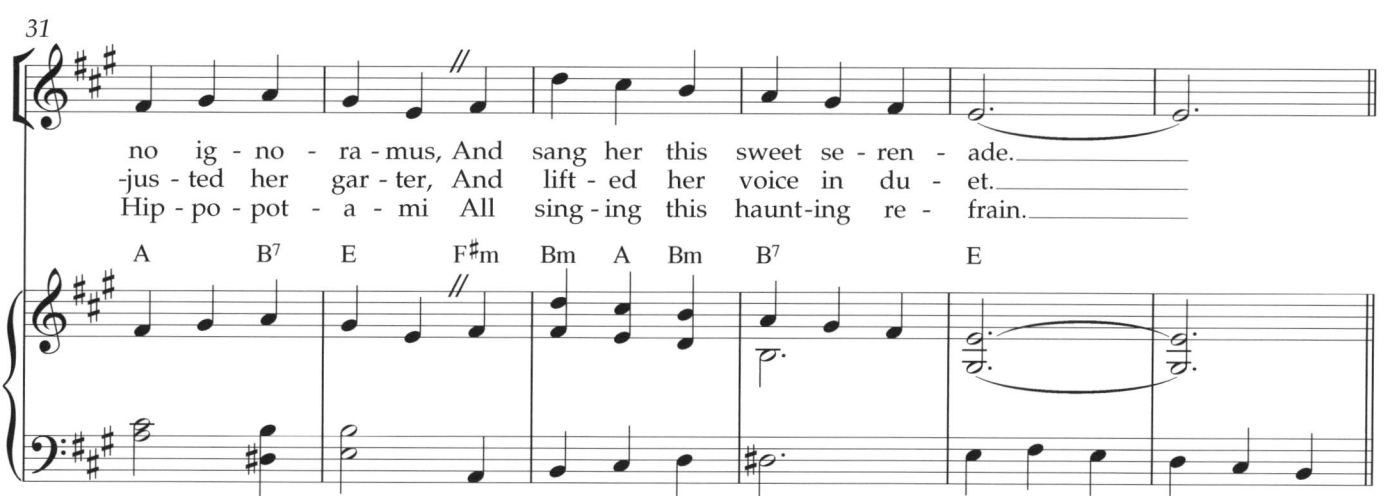

Feed the Birds

FOLDER 1
full performance 19
backing only 20

Words and Music by
Richard Sherman and Robert Sherman

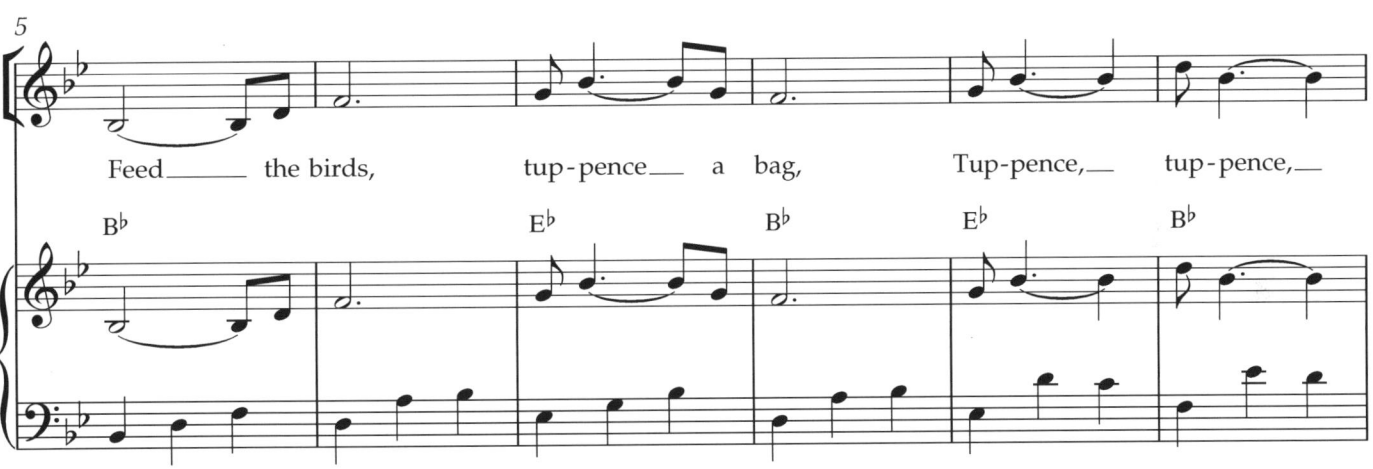

Feed___ the birds, tup-pence___ a bag, Tup-pence,___ tup-pence,___

tup-pence___ a bag. "Feed___ the birds", that's what she cries,

© 1964 Wonderland Music Company Inc
Warner/Chappell Artemis Music Ltd

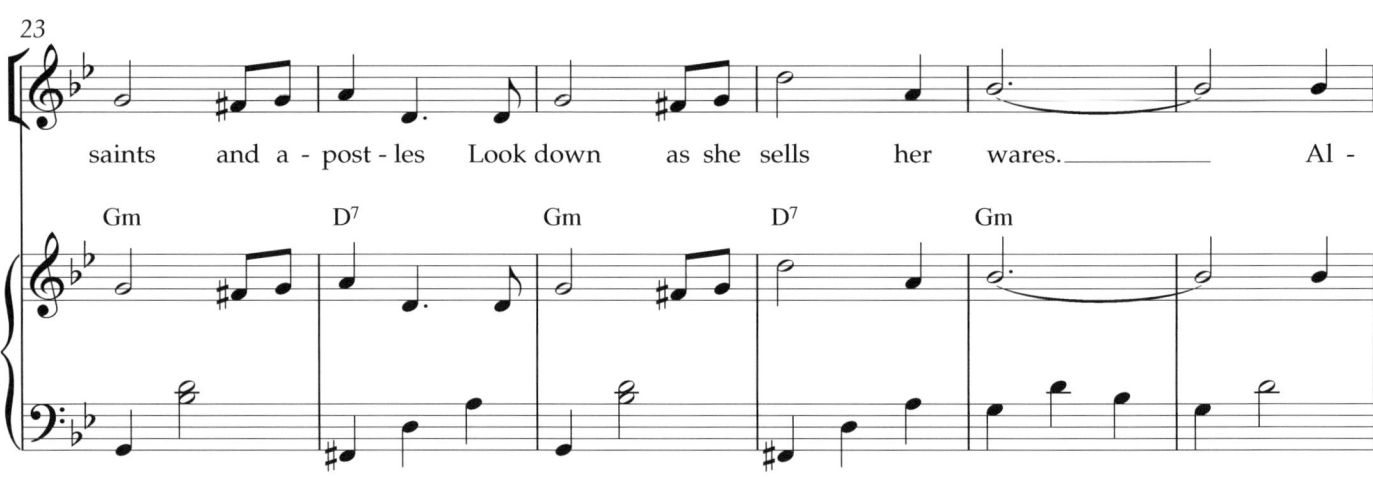

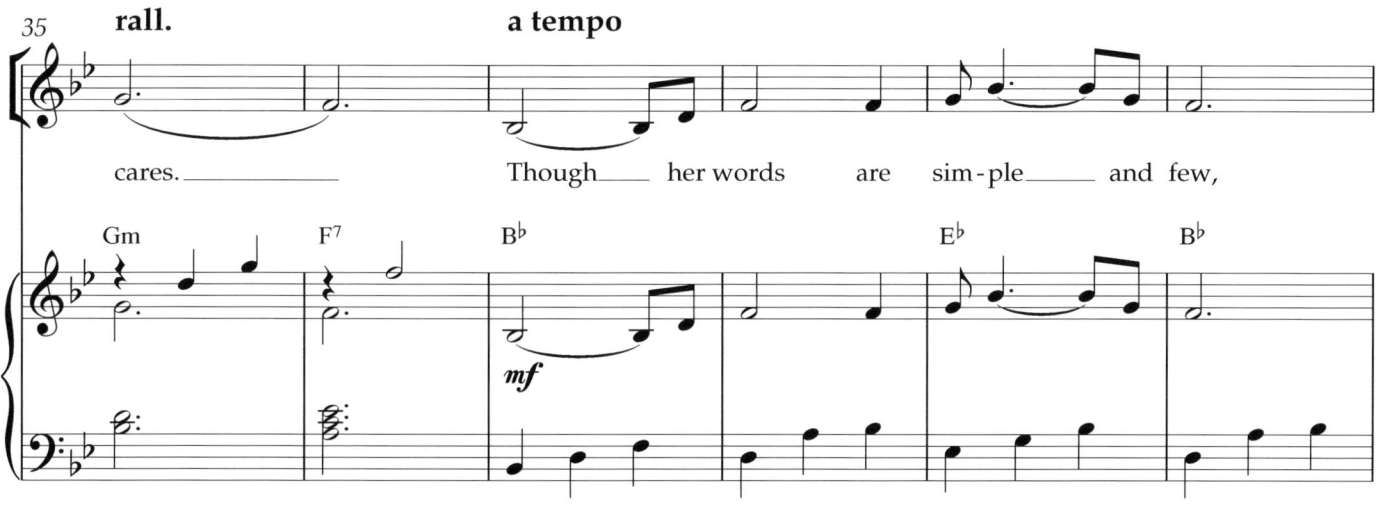

36

FOLDER 2
full performance [5]
backing only [6]

The Teddy Bears' Picnic

Words by Jimmy Kennedy
Music by John W. Bratton
arr. Lin Marsh

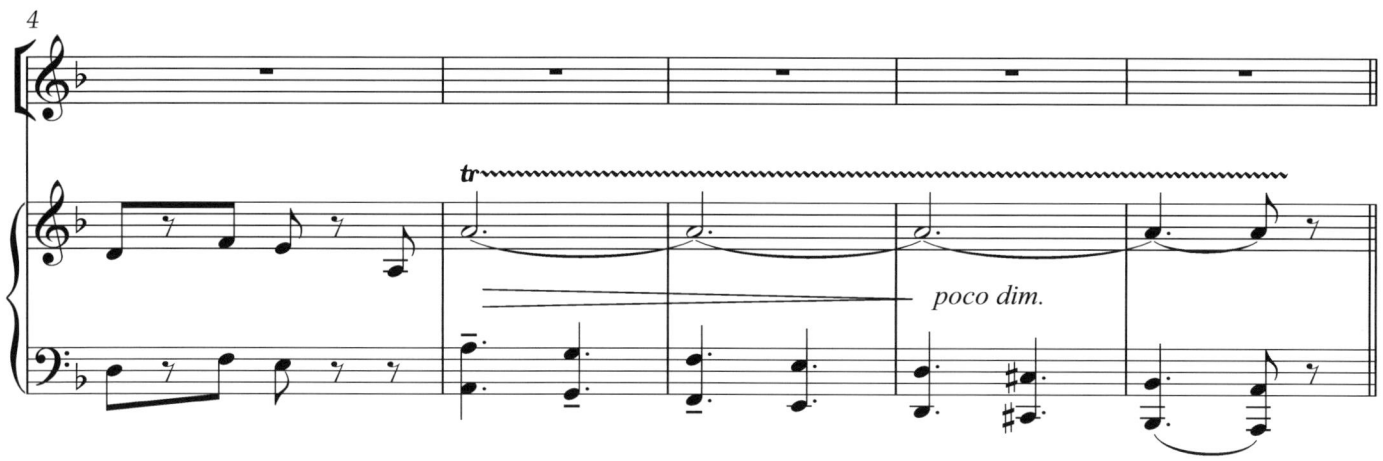

© 1907 M Witmark & Sons
B Feldman & Co Ltd

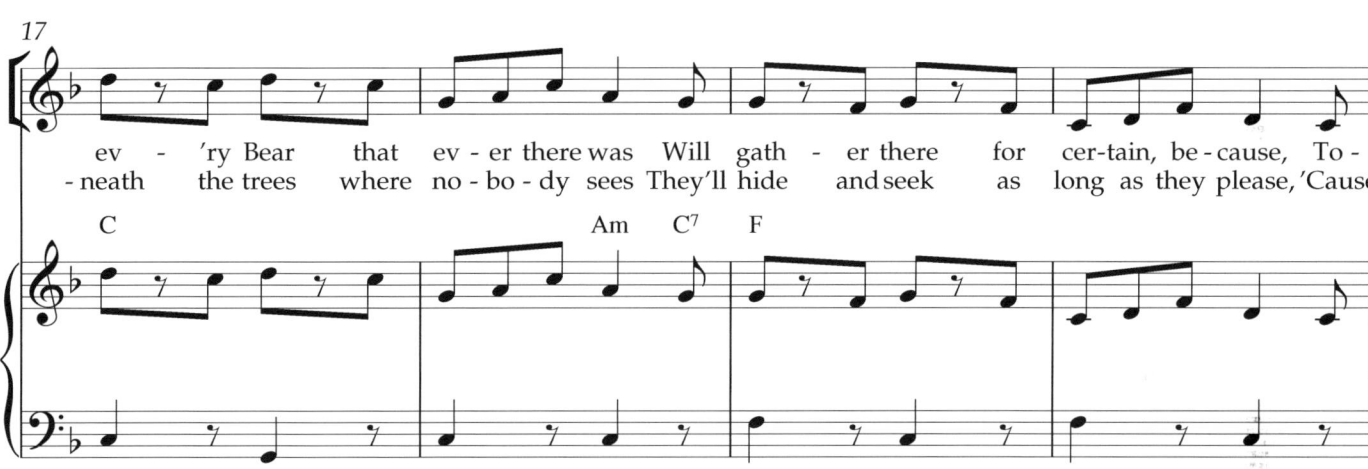

42

FOLDER 2

full performance [7]

backing only [8]

Nellie the Elephant

Words by Ralph Butler
Music by Peter Hart
arr. Lin Marsh

1. To Bom - bay a tra - vel - ling cir - cus came, they
2. Night by night, she danced at the cir - cus band, when

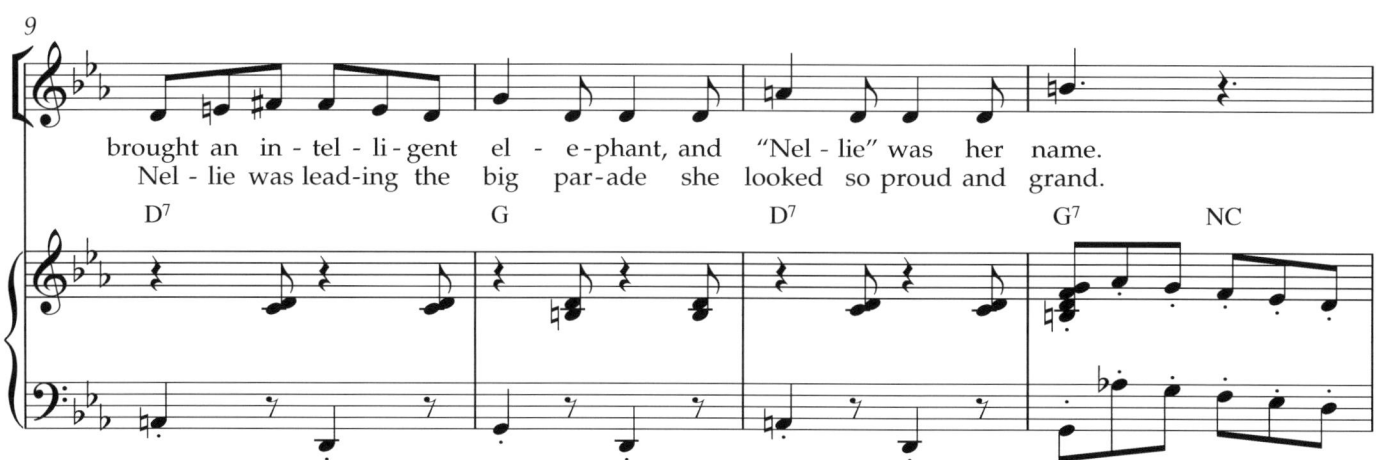

brought an in - tel - li - gent el - e - phant, and "Nel - lie" was her name.
Nel - lie was lead - ing the big par - ade she looked so proud and grand.

© 1956 Dash Music Co Ltd

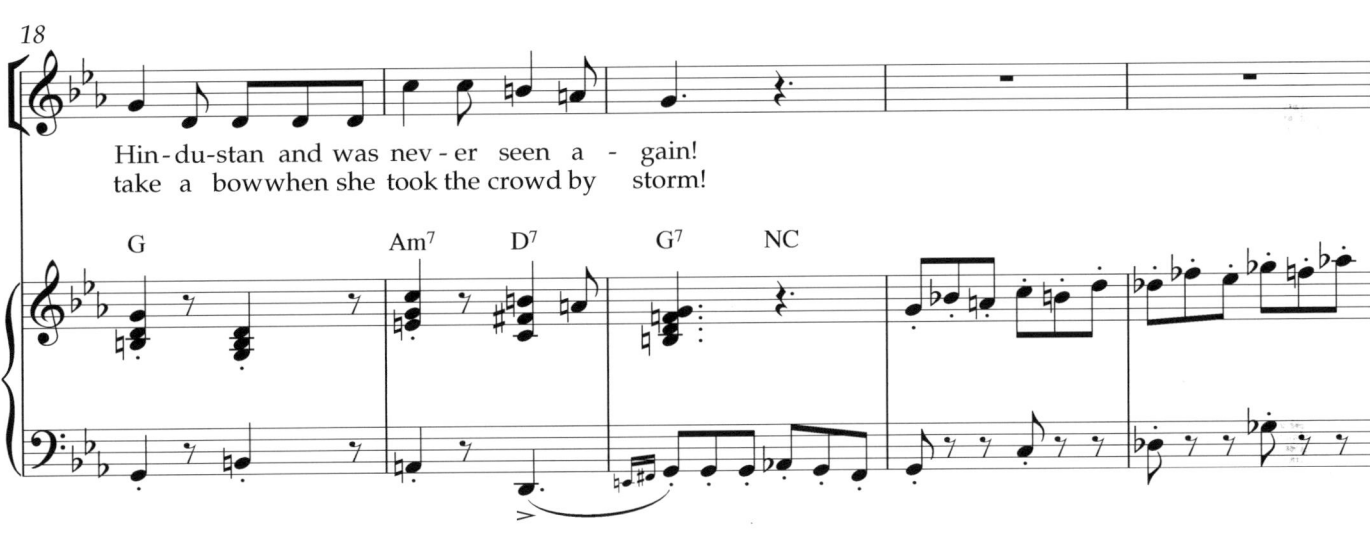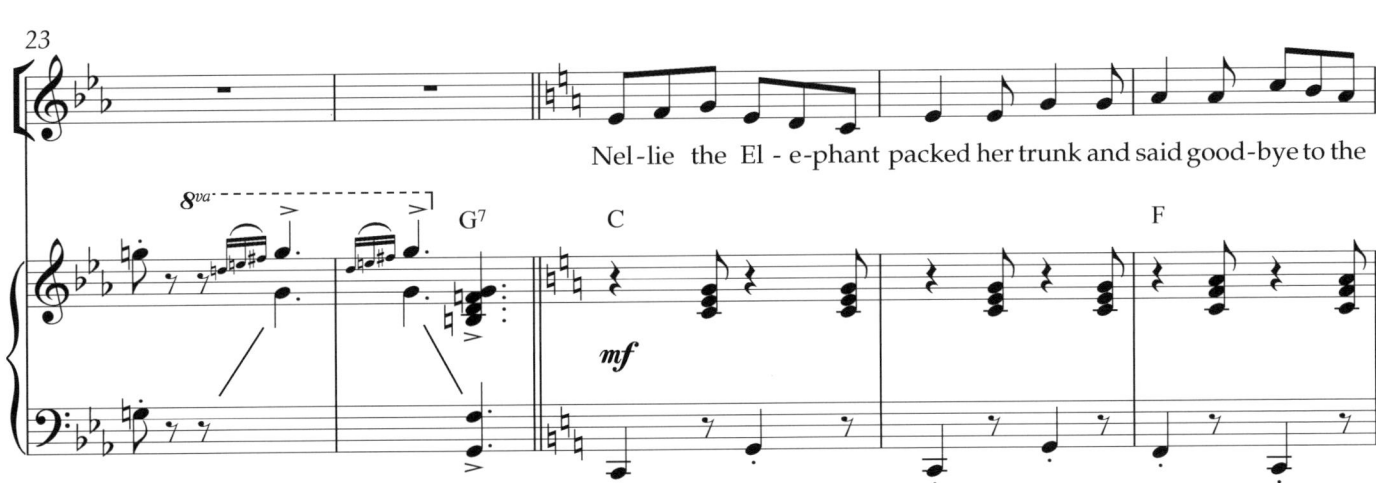

Going to the Zoo

Words and Music by Tom Paxton
arr. Lin Marsh

Brightly ♩ = 132

1. Dad-dy's ta-king us to the zoo to-mor-row, zoo to-mor-row, zoo to-mor-row.
2. See the el-e-phant with the long trunk swing-ing, great big ears and long trunk swing-ing.

Dad-dy's ta-king us to the zoo to-mor-row, We can stay all
Sniff-ing up pea-nuts with the long trunk swing-ing, We can stay all

day.
day. } We're go-ing to the zoo, zoo, zoo. How a-bout

© 1964 Cherry Lane Music Publishing Company Inc
Harmony Music Ltd

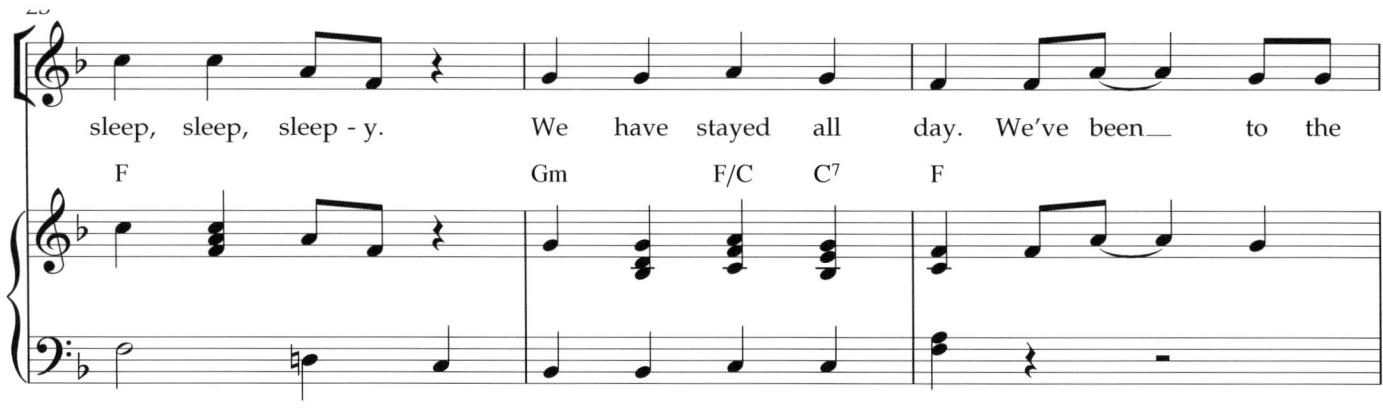

3. See all the monkeys scritch-scritch-scratching,
   Jumping all around and scritch-scritch-scratching,
   Hanging by their tails and scritch-scritch-scratching.
   We can stay all day.
   CHORUS

4. See all the seals honk-honk-honking,
   Catching fish and honk-honk-honking,
   Swimming in the pool and honk-honk-honking.
   We can stay all day.
   CHORUS

5. See music

6. Momma's taking us to the zoo tomorrow,
   Zoo tomorrow, zoo tomorrow.
   Momma's taking us to the zoo tomorrow,
   We can stay all day.
   CHORUS

The Runaway Train

FOLDER 2
full performance [11]
backing only [12]

Words and Music by Carson Robison
and Robert E. Massey
arr. Lin Marsh

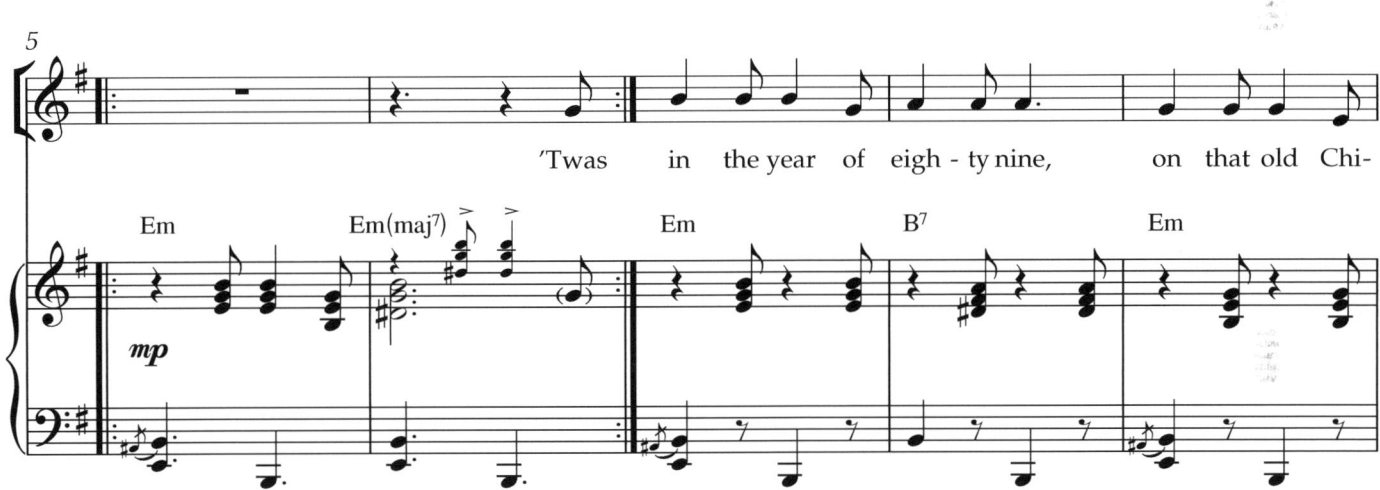

'Twas in the year of eigh-ty nine, on that old Chi-

-ca-go line, when the win-ter wind was blow-ing shrill; The

© 1931 Shapiro Bernstein & Co Inc
Shapiro Bernstein & Co Ltd

Swinging on a Star

Words by Johnny Burke
Music by Jimmy van Heusen
arr. Lin Marsh

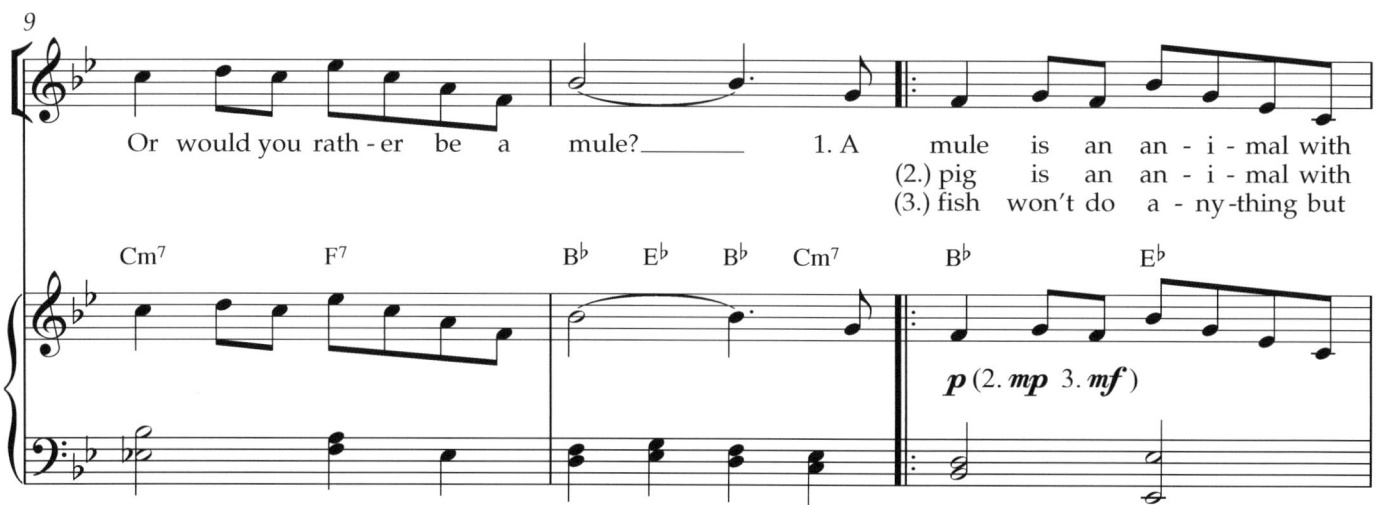

© 1957 Burke-Van-Heusen Inc
Chappell Morris Ltd

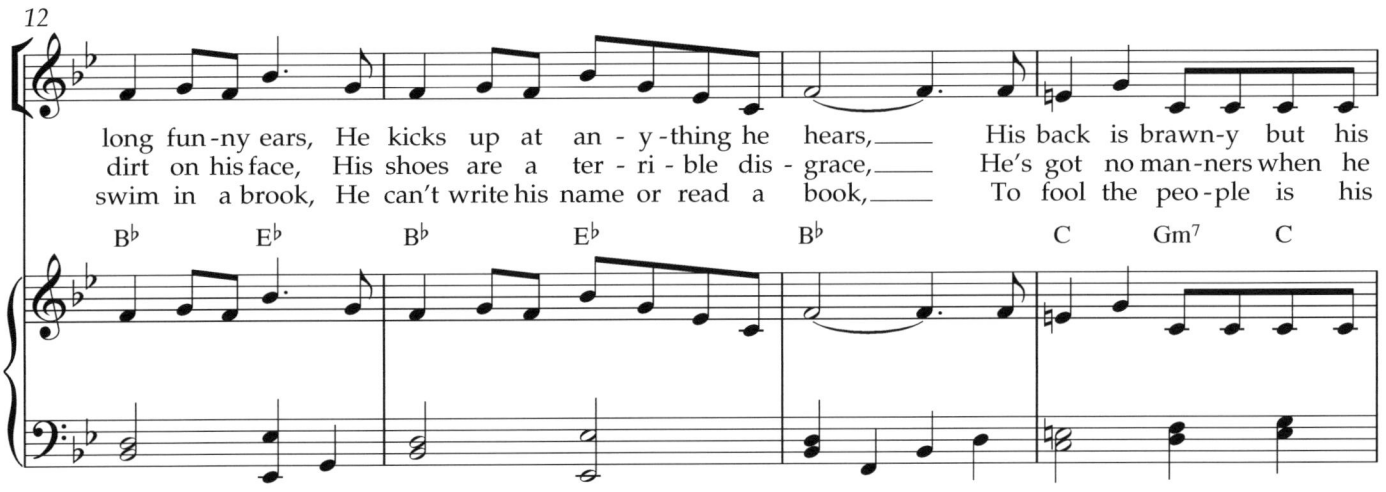

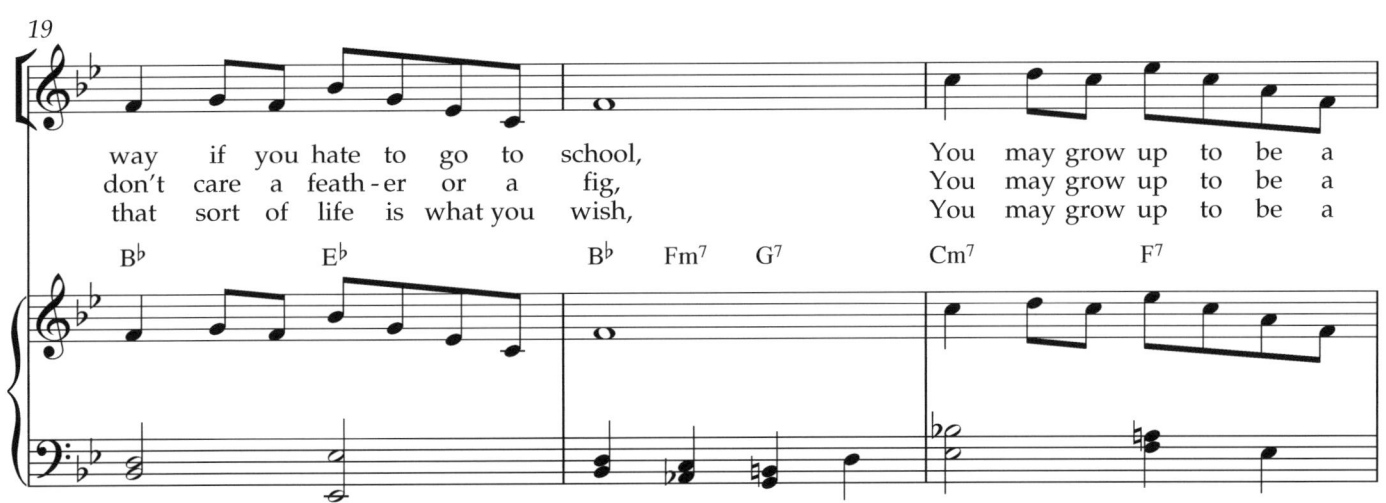

Two Little Men in a Flying Saucer

Words and Music by Arthur Pitt
arr. Lin Marsh

Two lit-tle men in a fly-ing sau-cer Flew round the world one day,

Looked to left and right of it, Could-n't bear the sight of it And quick-ly flew a-

© 1950 Cecil Lennox Ltd

Morningtown Ride

Words and Music by
Malvina Reynolds
arr. Lin Marsh

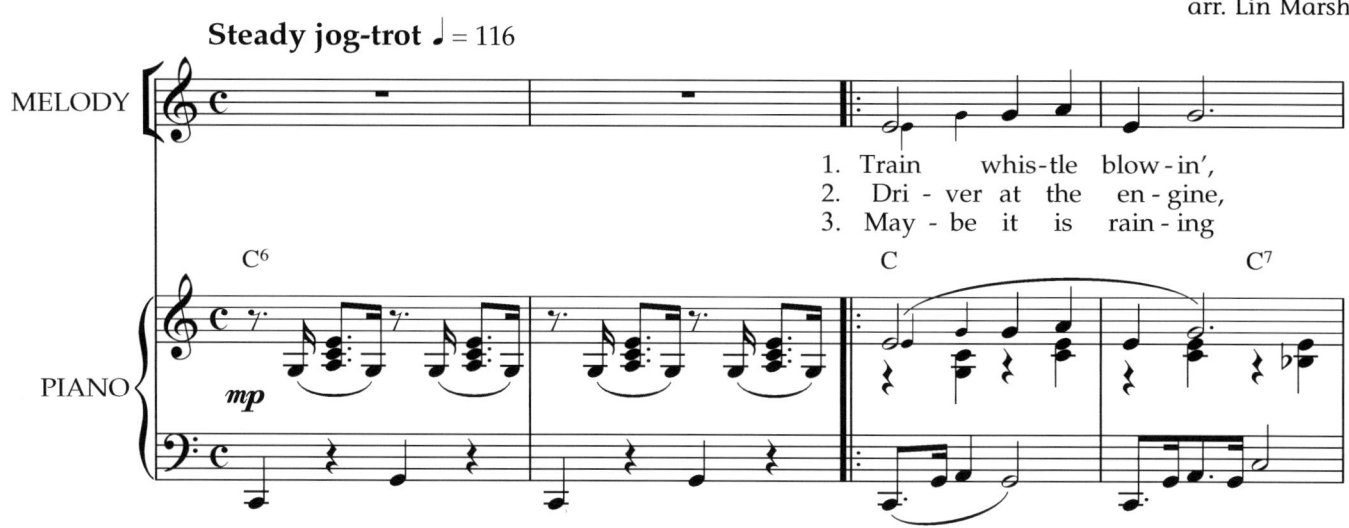

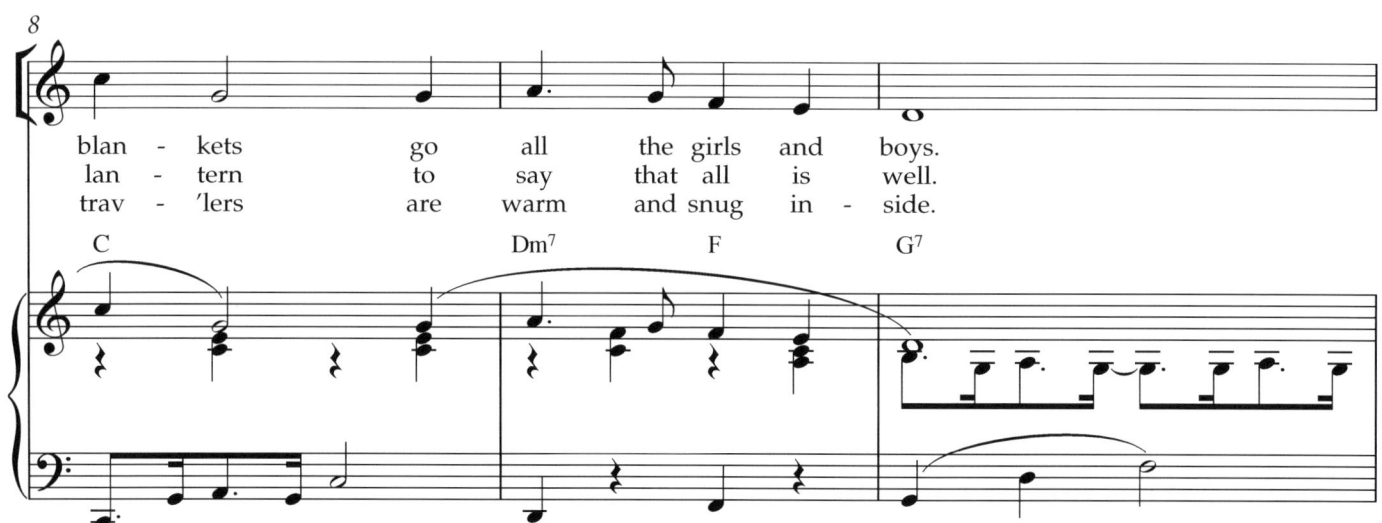

1. Train whistle blowin', makes a sleepy noise; underneath their blankets go all the girls and boys.
2. Driver at the engine, fireman rings the bell; sandman swings the lantern to say that all is well.
3. Maybe it is raining where our train will ride; all the little trav'lers are warm and snug inside.

© 1966 Amadeo-Brio Corporation Inc
MCS Music Ltd

Give a Little Whistle

FOLDER 2
full performance [19]
backing only [20]

Words by Ned Washington
Music by Leigh Harline

© 1940 Bourne Co.
Copyright Renewed
This Arrangement © Copyright 2008 by Bourne Co.
All Rights Reserved International Copyright Secured

THE SONGSCAPE SERIES
LIN MARSH

Key Stage 1–2

Junior Songscape (Book/CD)
ISBN: 0-571-52077-4

Junior Songscape: Earth, Sea & Sky (Book/CD)
ISBN: 0-571-52206-8

Junior Songscape: Stage & Screen (Book/CD)
ISBN: 0-571-52503-2

Junior Songscape: Children's Favourites (+ online audio)
ISBN: 0-571-52644-6

Key Stage 3

Songscape (pupil's book)
ISBN: 0-571-51866-4   10-pack: ISBN: 0-571-51944-X

Songscape (teacher's book)
ISBN: 0-571-51867-2

Songscape: Stage & Screen (Book/ECD)
ISBN: 0-571-52609-8

Songscape: Christmas (Book/2CDs)
ISBN: 0-571-52643-8

To buy Faber Music publications or to find out about the full range of titles available
please contact your local music retailer or Faber Music sales enquiries:

Faber Music Ltd, Burnt Mill, Elizabeth Way, Harlow CM20 2HX
Tel: +44 (0) 1279 82 89 82   Fax: +44 (0) 1279 82 89 83
sales@fabermusic.com   fabermusicstore.com